Translated by Annette Englander
Edited by Jeanette Green

Library of Congress Cataloging-in-Publication Data

Klettenheimer, Ingrid.
    Great paper folding projects / Ingrid Klettenheimer ; [translated
by Annette Englander].
        p.   cm.
    Portions translated from two works originally published in German:
Einfache Faltarbeiten bunt ausgestaltet, and Falten und Gestalten.
    Includes index.
    Summary: Presents instructions for making paper folding projects,
from simple animals to fairy tale scenes.
    ISBN 0-8069-8554-2
    1. Paper work—Juvenile literature.   [1. Paper work.
2. Handicraft.] I. Title.
TT870.K556   1992   91-46524
736′.98—dc20   CIP
                                    AC

10 9 8 7 6 5 4 3 2 1

English translation and editorial arrangement
© 1992 by Sterling Publishing Company
387 Park Avenue South, New York, N.Y. 10016
This book is comprised of portions taken from
the following titles originally published in German
Einfache Faltarbeiten bunt ausgestaltet © 1986 by
ALS-Verlag GmbH, Frankfurt/Main and *Falten und Gestalten*
© 1988 by ALS-Verlag GmbH, Frankfurt/Main
Distributed in Canada by Sterling Publishing
℅ Canadian Manda Group, P.O. Box 920, Station U
Toronto, Ontario, Canada M8Z 5P9
Distributed in Great Britain and Europe by Cassell PLC
Villiers House, 41/47 Strand, London WC2N 5JE
Distributed in Australia by Capricorn Link Ltd.
P.O. Box 665, Lane Cove, NSW 2066
Printed in Hong Kong
All rights reserved

Sterling ISBN 0-8069-8554-2

Front cover: Ducks and Swans Swimming (p. 62)
Back cover: Fanciful Caterpillars (p. 6)

Contents

Introduction

The paper folding projects in this book borrow from the Japanese art of origami. However, these projects and themes are decidedly Western. Until recently, most Westerners who practiced the art of paper folding had not attempted to fold complicated forms—timidly reserving them for Japanese artists. And for children under ten years, complicated origami techniques had seemed quite impossible to achieve.

But this book will show you how even kindergarten children can produce the easy paper folding forms like simple kites, sailboats, drinking cups, houses, baskets, or animals. With a few turns and folds, these easy forms can be transformed into a wide variety of finished shapes. This book will help inspire both adults and children to design paper creatures or montages of their own. Children will also enjoy making cat springs or witch's steps that can serve as bodies and limbs for various creations like worms in apples, crocodiles, or springy puppets.

But just knowing one or two forms, a classroom of children can create a forest full of pine trees, a chatter of squirrels, a tumble of turtles, a gathering of sailboats in a pond, or a medley of Bremen Town Musicians. The finished paper creations detailed in these pages will fill any child or adult with pride.

As with any skill, practice makes perfect. Children may begin to create simple objects and creatures as soon as they have learned to execute simple folds precisely. For the best results, always work on a smooth, hard, protected base. Do not attempt to fold in the air. And carefully crease each created fold with a fingernail or thumbnail. Also, corners and edges should meet perfectly.

When you continue working with folded objects, there should be no limit to your imagination. To make sure your paper folding projects succeed, let's clarify some basic terms and show you how to make simple folds:

For the **mountain fold**, fold the paper backwards as shown at the line marked with dashes and dots.

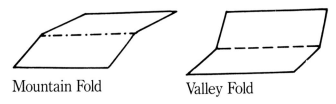

Mountain Fold   Valley Fold

For the **valley fold**, fold the paper forward as shown at the line with dashes only.

Changes in direction for an **inside fold** or an **outside fold** can be achieved when using paper folded longitudinally by *pre-creasing* the short diagonal. After that, the inside parts can be bent to the outside or the outside parts to the inside—depending on whether you pre-crease with a valley fold or a mountain fold. Either way, the results will be the same. In our illustration, the top figure when turned upside down is the same as the bottom figure.

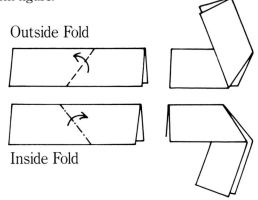

Outside Fold

Inside Fold

Mountain and valley folds are easier for young children than folds which require changes in direction or folding one end inside another. Whether or not you intend them to, each figure will have a certain individuality. All the penguins shown on p. 59, for instance, were made following the same paper folding directions (p. 58), but each penguin looks a little different than the next.

Two Basic Forms—Many Possibilities

In just four steps, you can create one of two basic forms (see illustration below). It is important that the paper, after the first two folding steps (folding the sheet into vertical, horizontal, and diagonal folds) is turned over and the same folds repeated on the reverse sides. The first two steps for basic form I and basic form II are identical. Then the sheet can be easily folded into the basic forms I and II. Many paper folding projects in this book utilize these basic forms. Although this book contains just a few possibilities, you will soon be able to invent new ways to use them.

Colorful Paper Blossoms   (p. 7)

One of each of the basic shapes folded and glued together make the colorful paper blossoms on the opposite page. Squares of wrapping paper with small patterns and col-orful origami 4-inch (10-cm) paper squares folded into shape partially cover the basic form I, which is in a solid color. Four leaf-shapes, folded longitudinally, then folded diagonally, are unfolded and bent outward to make the finished creation look more like a blossom. See the folding directions and leaf template on p. 8.

Fanciful Caterpillars   (back cover)

Make basic form II nine times to create the head, body, and tail of these caterpillars. For the head, a 4¾-inch (12-cm) paper square is needed. The six adjacent body parts are created out of 4-inch (10-cm) paper squares, and the tail is made from a 3¼-inch (8-cm) paper square. Glue together everything at one of the four valley folds, then shift the bottom parts a little while they are being glued so that it appears they are winding and twisting themselves as they move.

Make the eyes out of white and black self-adhesive stickers. Curl with scissors colorful paper strips for the tongue and tail. Then your caterpillar can move wherever you fancy.

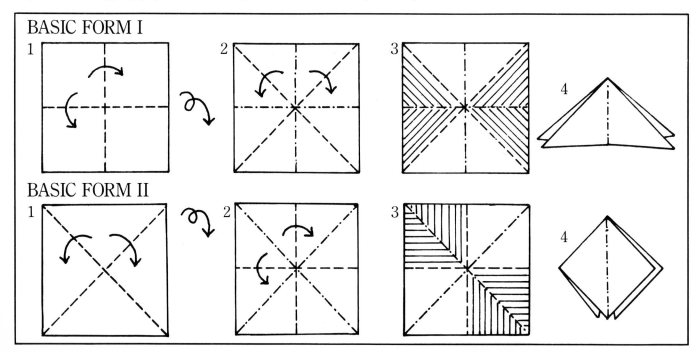

BASIC FORM I

BASIC FORM II

7 *Colorful Paper Blossoms* (p. 6)

COLORFUL PAPER BLOSSOM

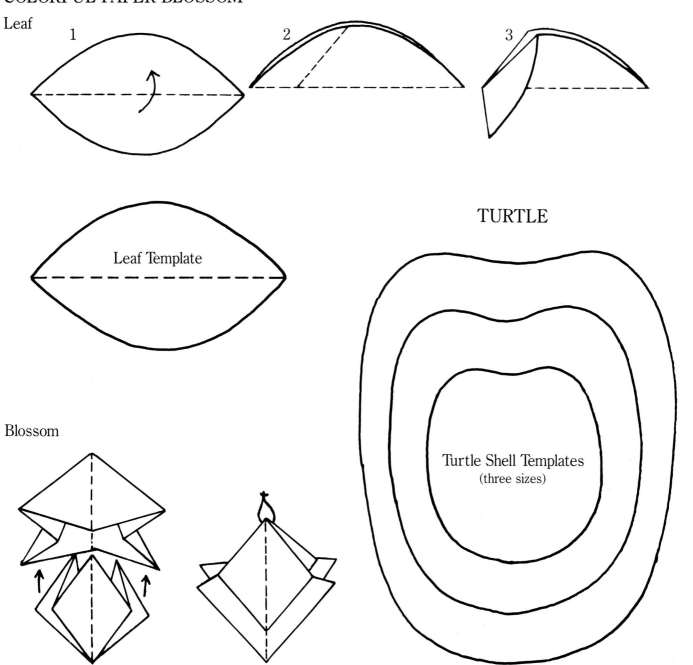

Leaf

1

2

3

Leaf Template

TURTLE

Turtle Shell Templates
(three sizes)

Blossom

SEAL

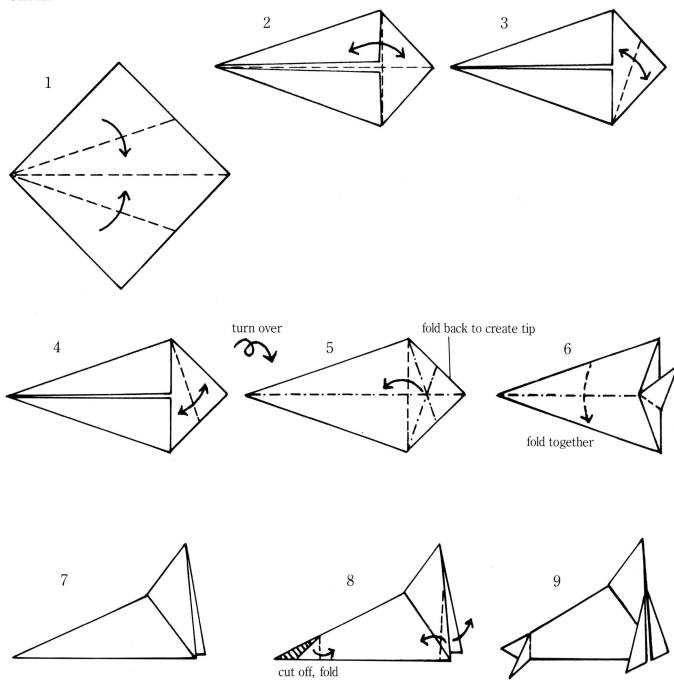

1

2

3

turn over

4

5   fold back to create tip

6

fold together

7

8   cut off, fold

9

Folded Animals

Since children enjoy creating three-dimensional animals, why not fold them out of paper? With a little help, when folds become tricky, elementary school children can make many of the animals shown and described here.

A Tumble of Turtles (p. 11)

It is mere child's play to make the turtles on the opposite page. They become most stable when they are made out of colored construction paper squares. The animals in the illustration are in three different sizes. The largest requires an 8-inch (20-cm) paper square, the medium a 6-inch (15-cm) square, and the smallest a 4-inch (10-cm) square. See folding instructions below. When you add a shell, the turtles appear especially real. Find patterns for three different sizes of shells on p. 8. Paint the shell in wood colors, and before you glue it on, bend the paper shell so that it arches up in the middle like a backbone.

A Circus of Seals (p. 12)

You can make these droll seals, which balance colorful paper balls on their snouts, quite easily out of 8-inch (20-cm) colored paper squares. See the illustrated folding directions on p. 9. The only slightly difficult steps are 5 and 6, folding the triangle for the head upwards. But after some practice, you can easily master these steps. Glue eight paper circles 1½ inches (4 cm) in diameter in two different colors together halfway and close them up to form balls, then stick the ball to the seal's snout with the aid of a pin.

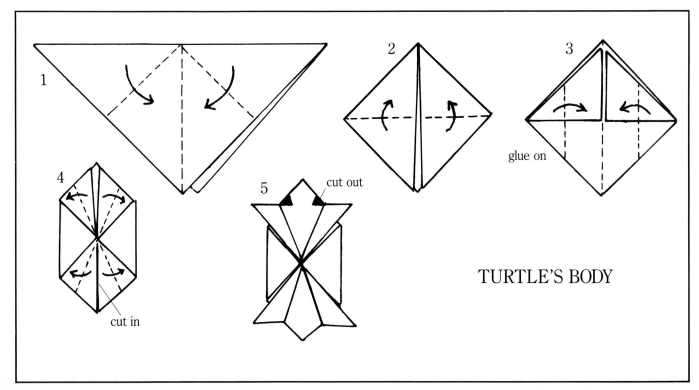

TURTLE'S BODY

11 *A Tumble of Turtles*   *(p. 10)*

A Circus of Seals   (p. 10)

13 *A Chatter of Squirrels* *(p. 14)*

A Chatter of Squirrels (p. 13)

Create these squirrels out of brown folding paper 8-inch (20-cm) or 6¾-inch (17-cm) squares. But you'll need some practice folding simpler forms before you try to fold a perfect squirrel. See folding instructions on p. 18. The triangles that point up (3), the corners folded in (4), and the ears and tail folds are a little tricky. But after a few tryouts, making them will become very easy.

In between the animals' cut-out paws they hold tiny pine cones or seeds. The squirrels on p. 13 chatter and romp around in a forest of pine trees. You'll find folding instructions for these pine trees on p. 19.

A Flutter of Butterflies (p. 15)

These delicate butterflies on the opposite page are best made from thin 6-inch (15-cm) paper, since shaping the little legs from thick paper would be difficult. Wrapping paper leftovers or pre-cut origami paper allow the butterflies to sparkle in summer colors. Follow the folding directions below. Cut their feelers out of tinted paper and glue them onto the head underneath the rudiments of wings.

The butterflies shown flutter in a meadow of colorful flowers. It is easy to create these flowers, though they take time. See flower folding directions on p. 19.

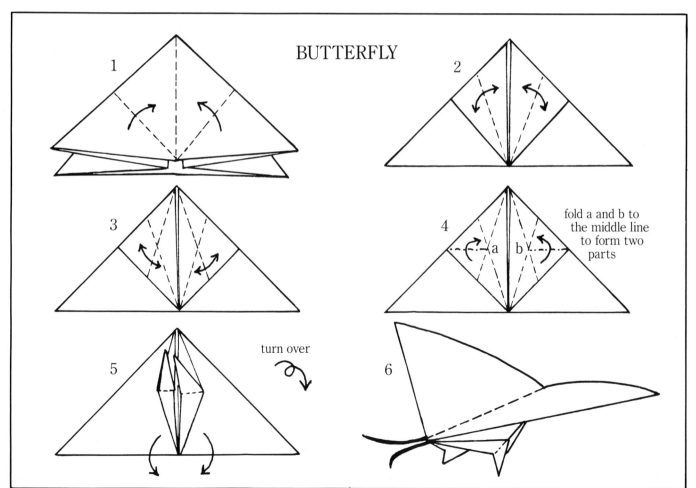

BUTTERFLY

1

2

3

4 — fold a and b to the middle line to form two parts

5 — turn over

6

14

15   *A Flutter of Butterflies*   (p. 14)

Little Star Baskets (p. 17)

These pretty little baskets can be, with a little folding experience, created by fourth-, fifth-, and sixth-graders. First, place the basic form II in front of you, so that the opening points up; then follow the step-by-step folding directions shown below.

It takes a little skill to give the basket its final shape. Use 11¾-inch (30-cm) colored paper squares, 8-inch (20-cm) square folding paper in strong colors, and 6-inch (15-cm) and 4-inch (10-cm) foil paper squares to make the basket collection shown on the opposite page. Self-adhesive star and angel shapes decorate the star basket's rays. You can fill them with colorful straw, excelsior, or goodies. These baskets could decorate party tables or even be used for Christmas, Easter, or other holiday treats.

Angels and Bells (p. 75)

Begin these angels and bells with basic form II (see p. 6). Then fold the two side corners toward the middle line, bend them up and back, and then fold back the part that juts out. This way you'll create the angel's gown or skirt. Begin with an 8-inch (20-cm) paper square. Find assembly directions for the angel's skirt and wings on p. 79.

To the bell-shaped angel skirts, add head, hair, and halo as well as wings. Insert wings made of foil between folds of the angel's gown. Hang the angels by a thin string. Find the templates for the angel's head, halo, and wings on p. 20.

When the four corners that point down are folded backwards and inward, the bell shape is completed. Gluing the bottom center bell parts together strengthens the bells and prevents them from losing shape. For these light

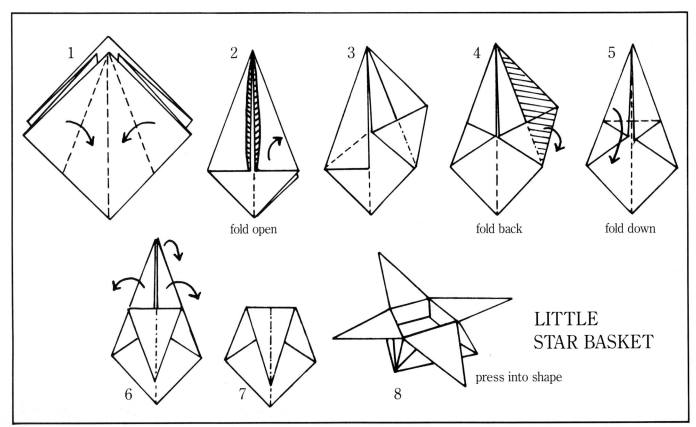

1

2   fold open

3

4   fold back

5   fold down

6

7

8   press into shape

LITTLE STAR BASKET

17 *Little Star Baskets* *(p. 18)*

SQUIRREL

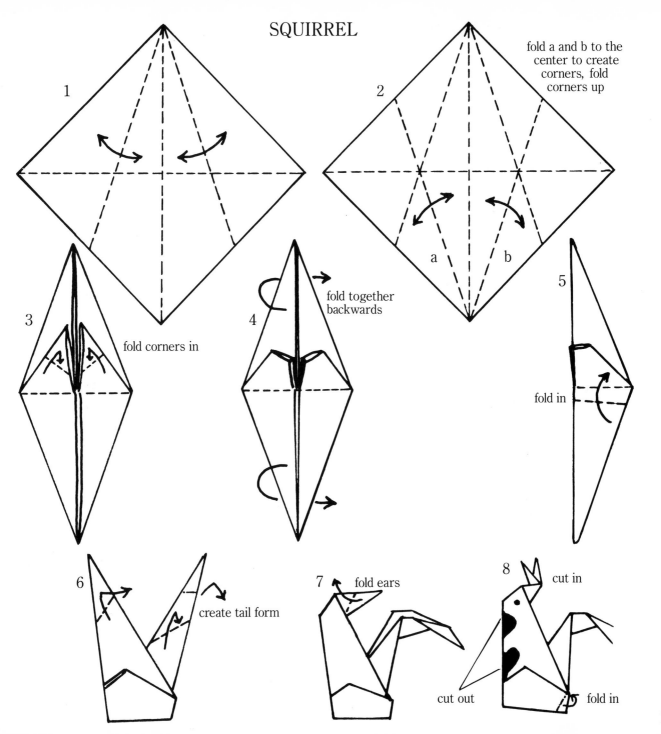

1

2 fold a and b to the center to create corners, fold corners up

a   b

3 fold corners in

4 fold together backwards

5 fold in

6 create tail form

7 fold ears

8 cut in

cut out   fold in

18

tree ornaments, use 6¾-inch- or 6-inch-square paper. Stick on self-adhesive stars to decorate the bells, and hang them on gold, nylon, or another thin string. See folding directions on p. 79.

Simple Pine Trees   (p. 74)

The simple paper pine trees, that sparkle in reds and purples on p. 74, consist of five basic form I's (see p. 6) glued on top of each other. You can make taller or shorter trees by overlapping individual parts a little more or a little less. The trees are most stable when you fold them out of strong tinted paper, like construction paper. Use assorted colors, and begin with the bottom, folded out of a 6-inch (15-cm) paper square, and fold each succeeding set of pine branches out of a square that's ¾ inch (2 cm) smaller than the previous one. The last folded paper square to crown the tree with a point will be a 2¾-inch (7-cm) paper square. Follow folding directions opposite.

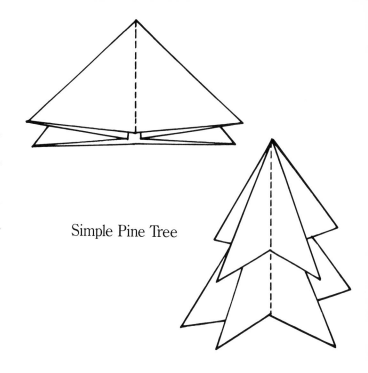

Simple Pine Tree

Skirt, Bell, and Pine Tree

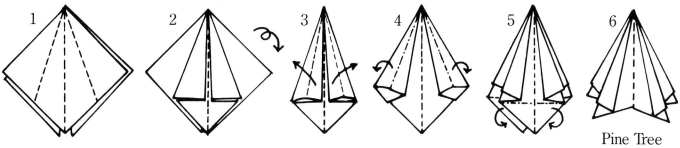

Pine Tree

Flower or Snow Cover for Pine Tree

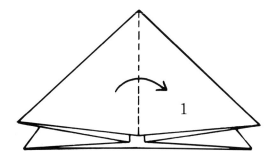 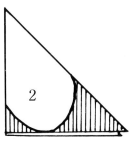 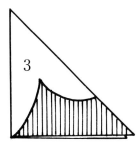

unfold, glue different forms on top of each other

cut out petal-shaped scallops for flower or color white paper green for snow-covered pine

19 FLOWER, SKIRT, AND PINE TREE VARIATIONS

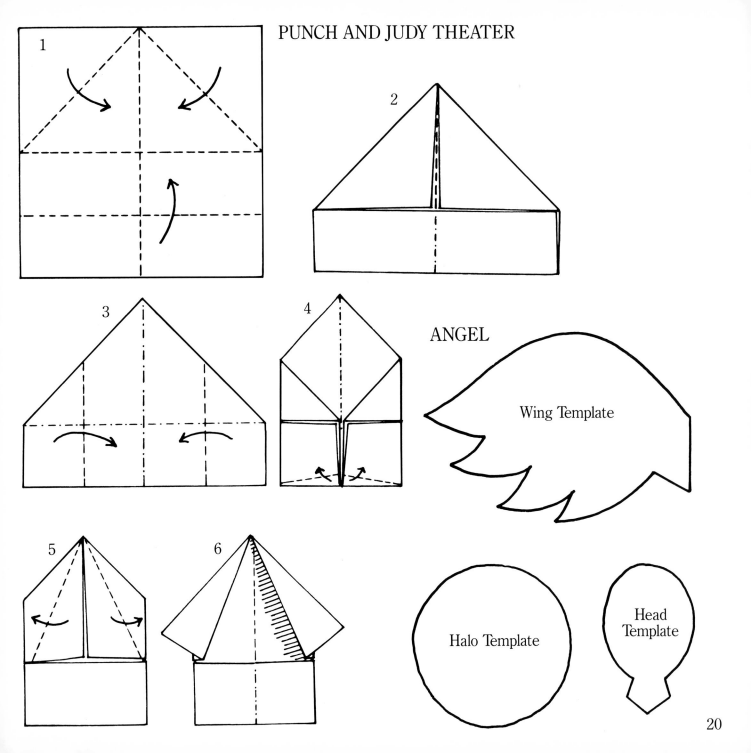

PUNCH AND JUDY THEATER

1

2

3

4

ANGEL

Wing Template

5

6

Halo Template

Head
Template

20

Potpourri for Children

These quickly made folding figures can be decorated, and they will delightfully fill children's free time in kindergarten or elementary school. Children will enthusiastically make this potpourri of folded paper crafts and these projects will stimulate them to make still more paper crafts. Here's a sampling of things they can make quite simply. They can put on their own Punch and Judy show, feed the birds, sail boats on a make-believe pond, and lie on the beach.

Punch and Judy Show   (p. 22)

Make a colorful theater for a traditional Punch and Judy show—or whatever show you choose—from 14-inch (35-cm) colored paper squares. Follow folding directions on p. 20. The last two steps involve folding small parts of the lower edge of the back up so that the theater will be stable, and turning up the diagonal parts of the curtain. Be careful with these folds. Kindergarten children folded and decorated the little theaters on p. 22. Add colorful patterns with crayons. Also, cut out some Punch and Judy characters drawn with felt-tip pens on file folders or lightweight cardboards. Attach them to the stage with glue in some spots. If you wish, add a white paper background to the stage so that the characters stand out brightly.

Little Bird Houses   (p. 23)

For the little bird houses on p. 23, fold the basic form I (see p. 6) out of 6-inch (15-cm) brown paper squares to form the roofs. And use strips of brown colored paper to complete the bird house construction. The little bird houses stand on blue letter-size paper with a white snowy landscape made out of drawing paper and glued onto the blue background. Paint the birds with felt-tip pens on drawing paper and then cut them out and glue them to the blue sheet. In the illustration on p. 23, children drew the bird beaks and legs directly onto the blue base. You can add real feathers for the bird's tail and real birdseed. Finally, draw on snowflakes with pastel crayons.

Sailboats with Crews   (p. 24)

The colorful sailboats on p. 24 can be quickly folded—just follow the folding directions shown below. Folding the boat's hull is somewhat difficult, but once you show children how and they understand the basic idea, they will soon be able to make boats without help. The boat's stern (the rear) was covered inside with a piece of tinted paper to enhance its stability. It is easier to glue the two flaps, which are folded backwards, on top of each other. That will make the boat even more stable.

For their sailboats, children can create a merry crew, made out of little paper or cardboard figures drawn with felt-tip pens or colored pencils on both sides. Use colorful paper strips to decorate the hull and add a paper flag.

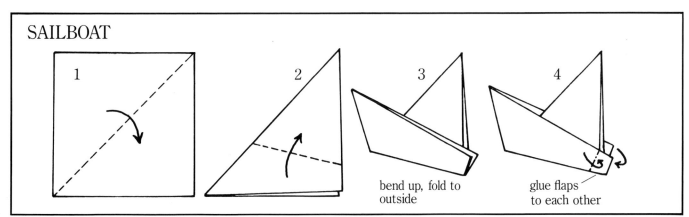

SAILBOAT

1

2

3
bend up, fold to outside

4
glue flaps to each other

Punch and Judy Show   *(p. 21)*

23　*Little Bird Houses*　(p. 21)

Sailboats with Crews   (p. 21)

25 *Beach Umbrellas and Sunbathers* *(p. 26)*

Beach Umbrellas and Sunbathers (p. 25)

The cheerful beach umbrellas, made from wrapping paper and construction paper, can be created from the basic form I (see p. 6). See folding directions on p. 28. The beach umbrella becomes stable when two umbrellas are glued on top of each other. Fold the upper umbrella out of a paper square that's ½ to ¾ inch (1 to 2 cm) smaller. This gives the umbrella an attractive, colorful rim. Begin with paper 6¼ to 9½ inches (16 cm to 24 cm) square.

Wrap a pointed beechwood stick with transparent tape underneath the top point of the umbrella; this way the umbrella pierced onto it will not slide off.

For the chaise longues, cut brown cardboard pieces 2 inches (5 cm) wide and 6 inches (15 cm) to 9½ inches (24 cm) long, and carve them with the aid of a ruler and a knife, leaving spaces, which may be copied from the folding directions on p. 28.

Once the two objects are folded into shape, glue them together at the ends. They're very stable, and in the illustration on p. 25, paper cutout sunbathers and towels lie on them.

Fairy Tale Scenes

Punch and Fairy Tale Characters (p. 27)

The lower parts of all characters on the opposite page are made from folded, but not glued, bell shapes. See folding directions for the bell-shaped skirts or gowns on p. 19. For **Little Red Riding Hood**, **Hansel**, and **Gretel** begin with 6-inch (15-cm)-square paper. For Hansel's pants and legs, push a green bell shape over a pink one; cut a triangle into both the front and back of the bell shapes at the same time. Fold 3-inch (7.5-cm) paper squares into basic form II to create the children's upper bodies. Use 2½-inch (6-cm) squares in facial color to create the heads. See p. 29 for folding and cutting directions. Use a 2-inch (5-cm)-square paper for Gretel's collar.

Make **Snow White**, **Punch**, the **Witch**, and the **Princess** from the Frog King tale from two bell shapes glued on top of each other and from one basic form II (see p. 6). Fold bell shapes out of an 8-inch (20-cm)-square paper and the basic form II from a 4-inch (10-cm)-square paper. Their heads should be somewhat bigger than those of the children, Hansel, Gretel, and Red Riding Hood (4-inch or 10-cm paper squares).

On the tip of the head, which is folded backwards (see folding directions on p. 29), attach paper strips for hair. Draw on facial features with colored pencils that can be used with water.

Create the hands of the small figures with paper strips folded into a loop and glued into the upper body parts. For Punch's arms and the Witch's kerchief, make basic form I, beginning with a 4-inch (10-cm) paper square. For the arms, cut basic form I through the middle. For the kerchief, just cut into basic form I, following directions on p. 29.

Create the Witch's hunchback where three corners of the upper body come together. Make the Witch's face in profile by folding two face parts forward and gluing them together after adding a large nose.

By cutting into the upper part of the body and folding it over, arm shapes can be created as seen in the Snow White character on the opposite page.

The folded cap or hood lets Little Red Riding Hood appear three-dimensional. Make the cap out of thin red 4-inch (10-cm)-square folding paper, following directions on p. 30. The little basket can be quickly made out of the drinking-cup shape (see p. 29).

Snow White holds in her hand a red wooden bead as an apple with a toothpick stem. The Princess from the fairy tale of the Frog King holds a ¾-inch (2-cm) cotton ball painted gold. The wrap for the Frog-King Princess and crowns—all made of gold foil paper—decorate the princesses.

Make Punch's cap out of a long paper triangle, folded in the middle, following the diagonal folds shown on p. 29, alternately folded to the inside and then bent outward, before you finally place the cap on Punch's head.

27 *Punch and Fairy Tale Characters*   (p. 26)

CHAISE LONGUE

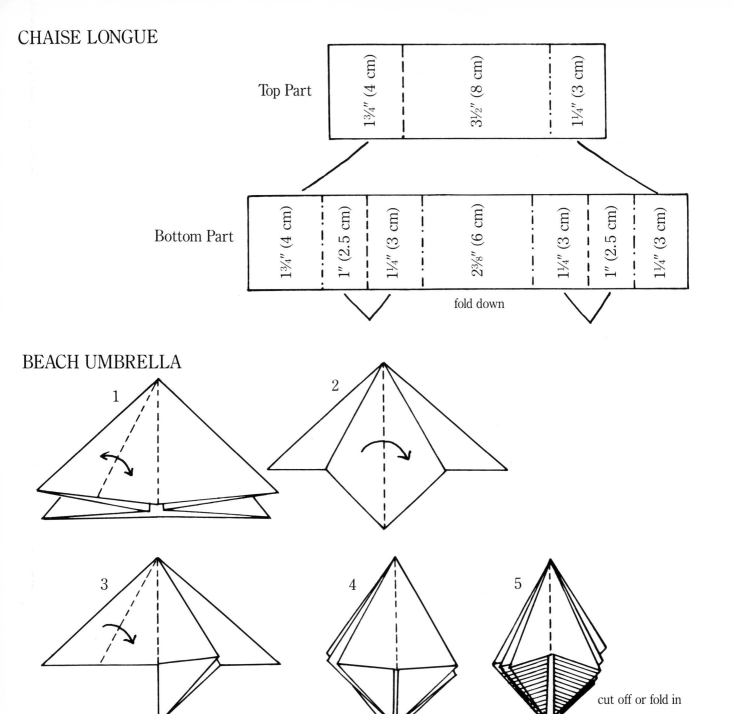

Top Part

1¾" (4 cm)   3½" (8 cm)   1¼" (3 cm)

Bottom Part

1¾" (4 cm)   1" (2.5 cm)   1¼" (3 cm)   2⅜" (6 cm)   1¼" (3 cm)   1" (2.5 cm)   1¼" (3 cm)

fold down

BEACH UMBRELLA

1

2

3

4

5

cut off or fold in

28

FAIRY TALE CHARACTERS

Red Riding Hood's Basket (Drinking Cup Form)

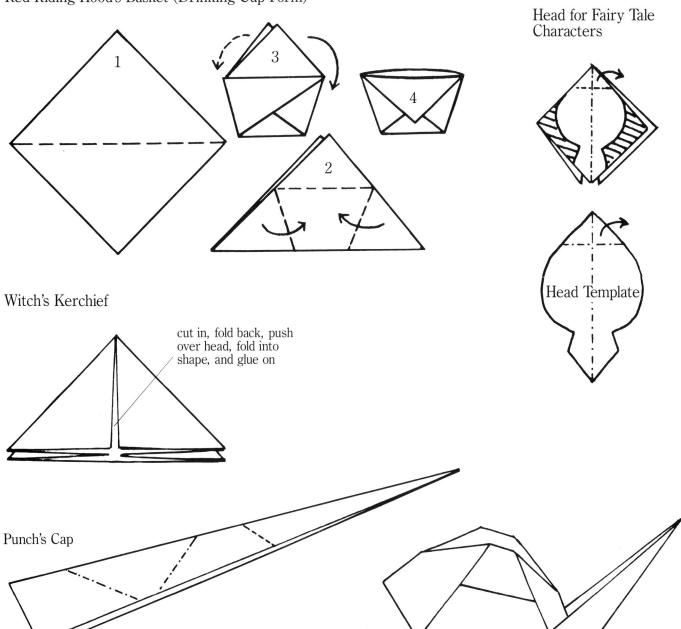

Head for Fairy Tale Characters

Head Template

Witch's Kerchief

cut in, fold back, push over head, fold into shape, and glue on

Punch's Cap

RED RIDING HOOD'S CAP AND SANTA'S SACK

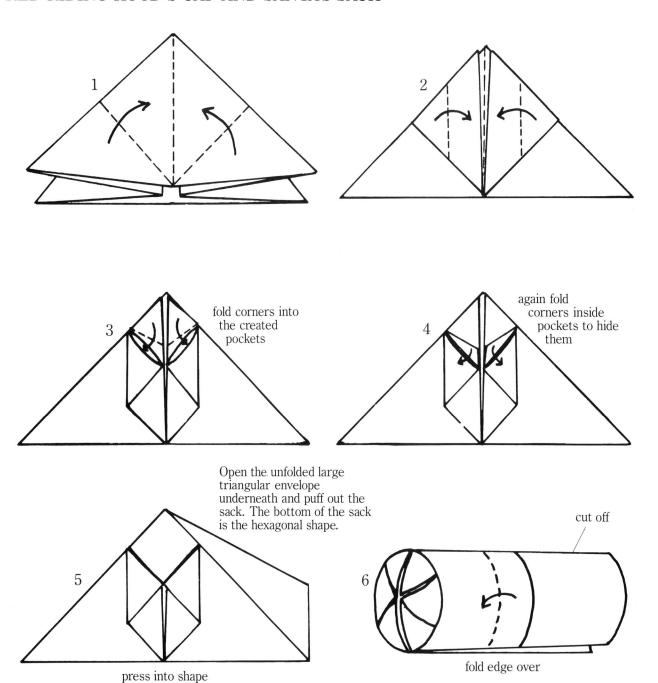

1

2

3 fold corners into the created pockets

4 again fold corners inside pockets to hide them

5 Open the unfolded large triangular envelope underneath and puff out the sack. The bottom of the sack is the hexagonal shape.

press into shape

6 cut off

fold edge over

WOLF

Body

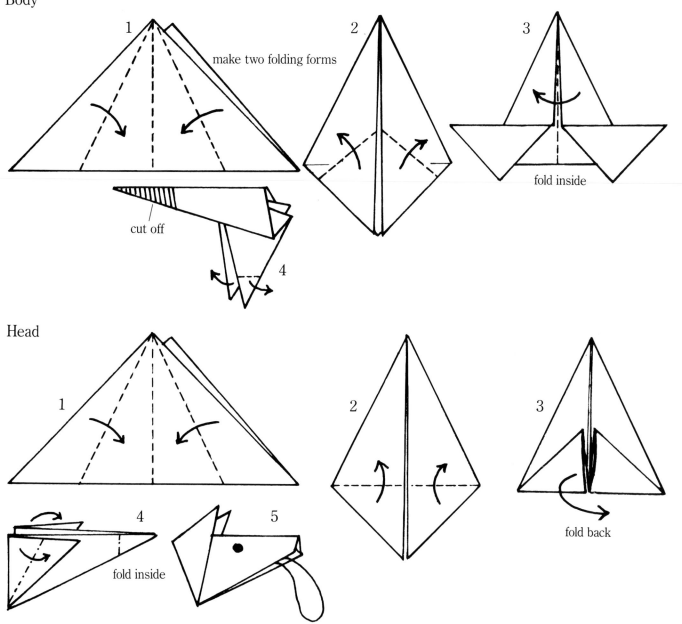

make two folding forms

cut off

fold inside

Head

1

2

3

4

5

fold inside

fold back

31

Red Riding Hood with the Wolf

Directions for folding Little Red Riding Hood are on p. 26. Make the wolf from three paper folding shapes, beginning with two 5½-inch (14-cm) squares for the body and one 3¼-inch (8-cm) square for the head. Follow the folding directions on p. 31. A red paper tongue and a brown paper fringed tail add the last touch.

The forest trees are made from bell shapes, glued onto each other. Use green folding paper squares in different sizes, beginning with a bottom paper square of 8 inches (20 cm) and a last treetop made from a 6-inch (15-cm) paper square.

The little mushrooms at the forest edge add a droll fairy tale appearance. Their stems are little white bell shapes made from 2½-inch or 3¼-inch (6-cm or 8-cm) paper squares. The mushroom tops can be made from patterned wrapping paper; begin with a 1¼-inch to 1¾-inch (3-cm to 4-cm) paper square in basic form I and glued onto white paper stems.

Red Riding Hood with the Wolf   (p. 32)

32

33   *Snow White and the Seven Dwarfs* (p. 34)

Snow White and the Seven Dwarfs (p. 33)

Snow White meets the seven Dwarfs in the same fairy tale forest where Red Riding Hood met the Wolf. You can use the pine trees and mushrooms over and over for new scenes. See folding directions on p. 19.

Folding directions for Snow White are on p. 26. Her friends, the dwarfs, are made from solid red or red-patterned paper squares. Each square is ¾ inch (2 cm) smaller than the previous one. Begin with a first square of 9½ inches (24 cm) and work down to a seventh square of 4¾ inches (12 cm). See folding directions below. Decorate the folded shapes with white, glued-on paper beards and faces folded down the center that form a right angle at the forehead.

The Princess and the Frog King (p. 35)

Questioningly, the little Princess looks at the Frog King, who wants to return with her to the castle. The frog sits on the edge of a pool or well, which originally was a little star basket (see folding directions on p. 16) made from 10¼-inch (26-cm)-square paper. The basket's spikes or star rays, however, were folded inward and glued on. The water in the well or pool is a 3¼-inch (8-cm) central square with 1½-inch (4-cm) side flaps cut out of light blue paper. Fold the frog out of a 4-inch paper square, following directions on p. 37. Add a very small crown made of gold foil paper, glue on paper eyes, and cut out a red paper mouth.

The colorful flowers that decorate the lawn can be created by cutting 3¼-inch (8-cm) and 2-inch (5-cm) paper squares, following folding directions on p. 19. Make the flower centers out of small self-adhesive yellow stickers that are also folded, so that the flowers appear three-dimensional.

Of course, you'll want to build the magnificent fairy tale castle shown on p. 35. Begin with a large (18-inch or 46-cm) drawing paper square decorated with red roofs made from 8-inch (20-cm) squares created in basic form I. Just add blue windows and a flag. The castle is very stable, a fairy tale delight. See folding directions for the white castle proper on p. 36.

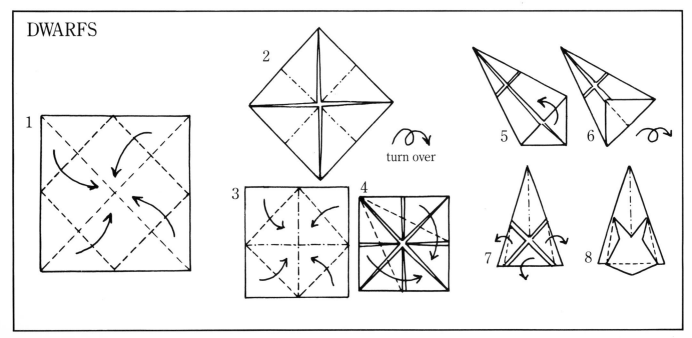

DWARFS

1 2 3 4 5 6 7 8

turn over

35 *The Princess and the Frog King* (p. 34)

FAIRY TALE CASTLE

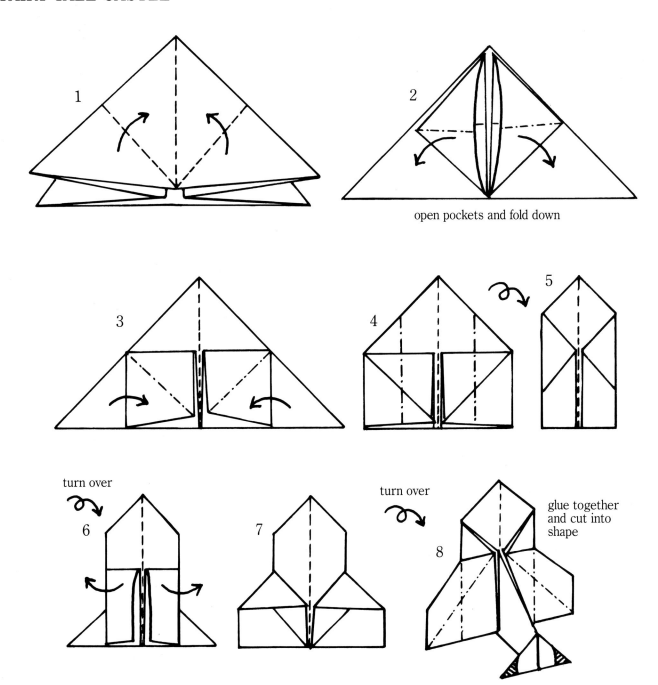

2 open pockets and fold down

5

turn over

6

turn over

8 glue together and cut into shape

Hansel and Gretel with the Witch (p. 41)

Here's a favorite Grimm fairy tale scene drawn from a popular German oral folktale commonly told in the 18th century. For the Hansel and Gretel scene in the forest in front of the gingerbread house, follow folding directions for fairy tale characters on p. 26. For the pine trees and mushrooms, see folding directions on pp. 19 and 32. Fold the witch's house out of 18-inch (46-cm)-square-patterned wrapping paper following folding directions on p. 38. The roof is also made from wrapping paper. Use an 8-inch (20-cm) paper square; fold it into basic form I, and glue it on. Make the chimney from a tiny house form, attached to the roof upside down. Add paper windows and doors to finish the gingerbread house.

FROG KING

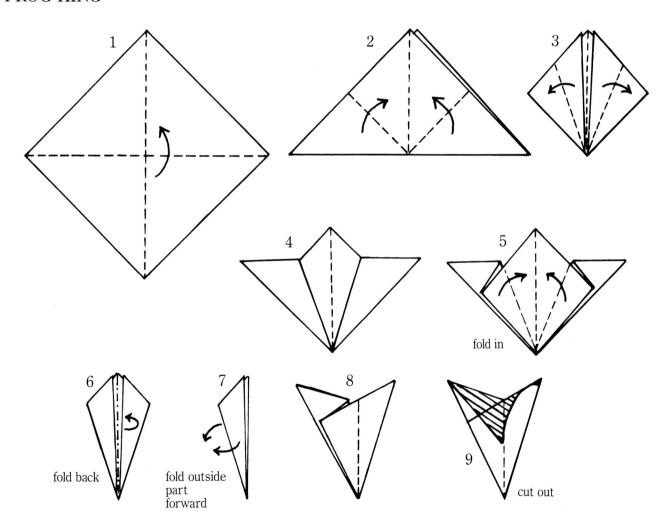

The Pied Piper of Hamelin (p. 39)

In this wintry scene, the Pied Piper of Hamelin leaves the town, with rats following him. The rats clearly stand out against the white ground and bustle about the feet of the Pied Piper. The Pied Piper's gown is made from colored 8-inch (20-cm)-square paper and the cape from green 6-inch (15-cm)-square paper. Make the head and hat out of a brown 5½-inch (14-cm) paper square. See folding directions on p. 40. Cover the face on both sides with a skin-color paper. It takes time and patience to make this figure, but once your Pied Piper has his beard, feather in his cap, arms, and a flute made of rolled-up silver foil, he's a fine-looking, stable chap.

The rats can be quite easily folded. Painted-on eyes and a long paper tail add the last touch. Make the rats out of 2¾-inch (7-cm) or 4-inch (10-cm) folded paper squares in whatever color you choose.

Make the houses in the town of Hamelin the same way as the Witch's house in Hansel and Gretel, following the directions below. You'll need 19-inch (48-cm), 18-inch (46-cm), or 16½-inch (42-cm) wrapping paper squares. Create the roofs from 8¾-inch (22-cm), 8-inch (20-cm), 7½-inch (19-cm), and 7-inch (18-cm) paper squares, using basic form I. See folding directions for the wintry pine trees on p. 19.

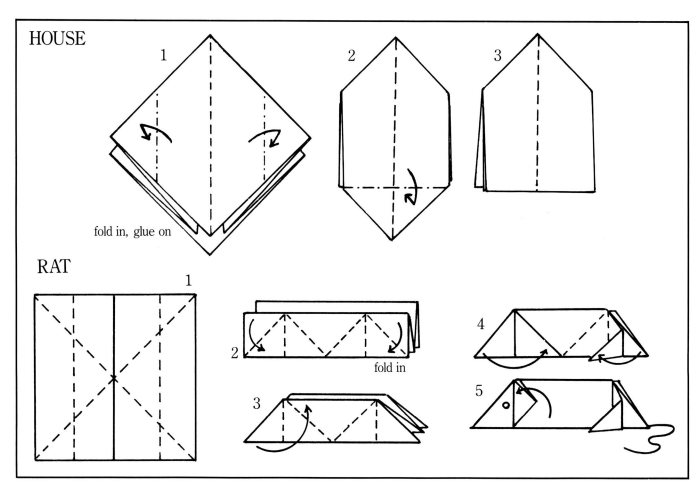

HOUSE

1   2   3

fold in, glue on

RAT

1

2   fold in

3

4

5

38

The Pied Piper of Hamelin (p. 38)

PIED PIPER

Head

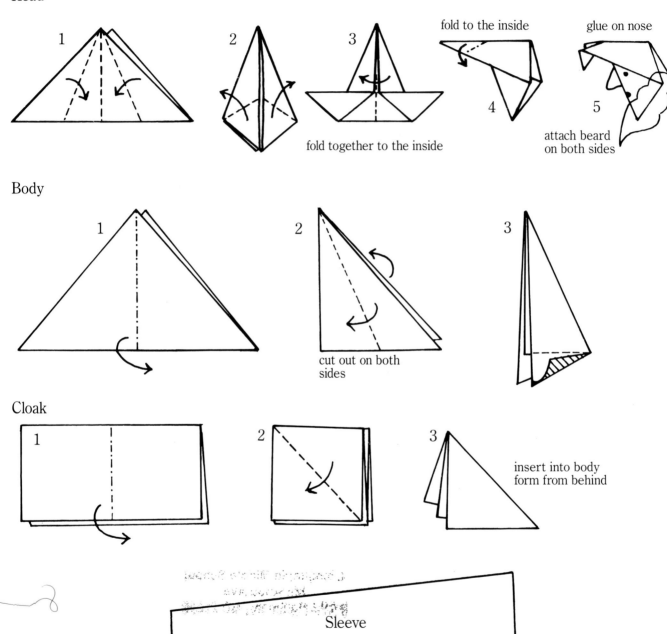

1

2
fold together to the inside

3

fold to the inside

4

glue on nose

5

attach beard
on both sides

Body

1

2
cut out on both
sides

3

Cloak

1

2

3
insert into body
form from behind

Sleeve

40

41 *Hansel and Gretel with the Witch*   (p. 37)

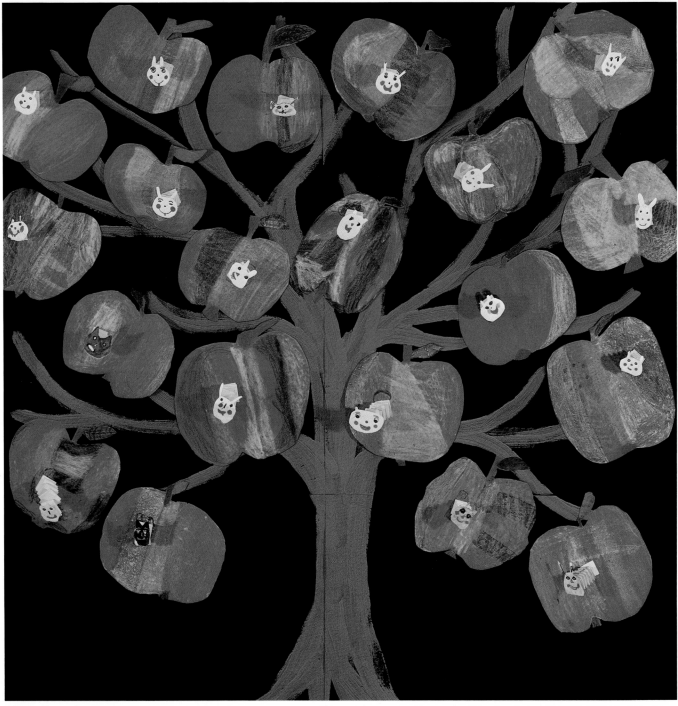

Apple Tree with Worms   (p. 43)

Cat Springs

The folding procedure for cat springs (witch's steps) is quite simple. But children may have difficulty, especially with long paper strips, trying to stick to right angles and to crease every fold carefully. That means that the witch's steps will turn out somewhat crooked, which will not reduce the figure's stability but does add a lively effect.

Apple Tree with Worms   (p. 42)

The apple tree on the opposite page with a worm in every apple was made by first-graders. The worms are cat springs (witch's steps) made from long, yellow construction paper strips ¾ inch by 10 inches (2 cm by 25 cm). Paper faces were added to the front tips of the worms, which wobble back and forth on the apples.

Octopuses, Punch Puppets, and Pipe-Cleaner People   (p. 44)

Use two beverage coasters with holes and covered with colored paper to make the octopuses. The six legs each consist of cat springs; the measurements for the folding strips are ¾ inches by 20 inches (2 cm by 50 cm). Use ribbons to attach the parts, add a paper face, and hang them by ribbons. Find the head template on p. 52.

The arms and legs of the punch puppets are also made of long paper cat springs—2 inches by 20 inches (5 cm by 50 cm). Cut out a large round paper head shape and neck. Add hair and facial features made from construction paper. Attach cutout paper shoes and hands.

Make the pipe-cleaner people out of two braiding strips ¾ inch by 20 inches (2 cm by 50 cm), pierced at top and bottom twice each for legs and head. Tie on bast fibre or string to create their hairstyles.

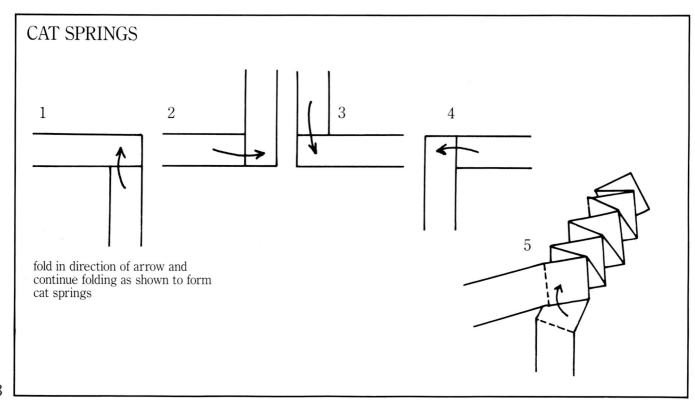

CAT SPRINGS

1   2   3   4

fold in direction of arrow and
continue folding as shown to form
cat springs

5

Octopuses, Punch Puppets, and Pipe-Cleaner People   (p. 43)

44

Paper Crocodiles (p. 45)

The paper crocodiles below are made of four long paper strips 2¼ inches by 20 inches (6 cm by 50 cm) for the body. Allow two of them to come to a point at one end. Fold the four legs out of ¾-inch-by-20-inch (2-cm-by-50-cm) paper strips. Create upper and lower jaws from the pattern on p. 53. Cut out white paper teeth and green paper paws. Add white cotton-ball eyes with black pupils to complete these eerie fellows. Now they are ready for wriggly play. They move with accordion steps and their big jaws snap open and shut at passing prey.

Simple Folded Objects

Some very simple paper folding objects easily made by kindergarten children are the kite, simple folding house, and simple folding boat.

Children Flying Kites   (p. 47)

For the illustration of children flying kites on the opposite page, kindergartners folded 4-inch (10-cm) paper squares into the kite form and made kite faces and tails from colored paper cutouts. See kite folding directions below. They drew themselves with crayons on white letter-size drawing paper. The cutout figures finally were grouped together for a wall picture on black construction paper with the kites and strings.

Simple Folded Houses   (pp. 48 and 49)

The simple folded houses can be drawn or painted and set up (as for the town on p. 49), or they can be used as the basic shape for a creative project (like that on p. 48). See folding directions on this page below.

Of course, these two craftworks are a little more difficult than the simple kites and require some perseverance. The town of simple folded houses can be used in many different ways and painted all around with windows, doors, and flowers. The houses easily stand by themselves.

The simple folded house form made into a school is used for the illustration School's Out! shown on p. 48. With colorful felt-tip pens, second-graders designed the gangs of children who gleefully run out of the school.

Lake with Simple Folded Sailboats   (p. 50)

A kindergarten class created the simple folded sailboats on p. 50. The sailboats float on a paper blue lake which sits on a patterned carpet. The boats are made out of white 12-inch (30-cm) and 8¼-inch (21-cm) drawing-paper squares. With the aid of thick, colored felt-tip pens, the children supplied a merry crew. The same sailboat form was used for the boats in the lower right corner of the Holland scene on p. 68. See folding directions for these simple folded sailboats below.

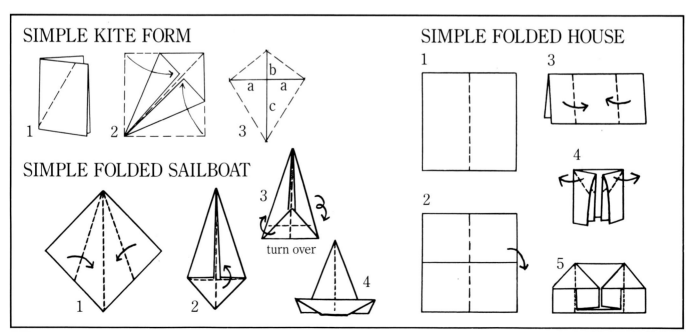

SIMPLE KITE FORM

SIMPLE FOLDED HOUSE

SIMPLE FOLDED SAILBOAT

turn over

47 *Children Flying Kites* *(p. 46)*

School's Out! (p. 46)

49   *Town of Simple Folded Houses*   (p. 46)

Lake with Simple Folded Sailboats   *(p. 46)*

Folded Boats

The simple boat is one of the best-known paper-folding forms and can become a part of many creative tasks. See examples on pp. 55, 56, and 68.

The Brave Tin Soldier   (p. 54)

The fairy tale of the Brave Tin Soldier by Hans Christian Andersen inspired the children's pictures on p. 54. Against the background of blue letter-size paper with a wavy sea is the small folded boat form. The characters of the dancer and tin soldier were drawn, cut out, and glued inside the little ships.

Landscape with Lake   (p. 55)

Follow folding directions for the simple boat below.

Clacking Heads   (p. 57)

The simple boat form is almost unrecognizable in the clacking heads on p. 57. For this easily folded form, simply bend the sail surface over at the end, and fold the "boat" together above its bottom part. If you also fold the upper and lower points in, the basic shape is completed. The clacking heads shown on p. 57 were decorated with colored construction paper, but they can also easily be painted with felt-tip pens. In the illustration on p. 57, they're attached to soft-drink bottlenecks.

Boat Harbor   (p. 56)

For the large folded boats shown in the boat harbor scene on p. 56, fold a large rectangular piece of paper lengthwise, open it up, and fold it in along the long side up to the center. Follow folding directions on p. 52. Now turn the sheet over and divide it into different directions by folding a and c onto d and b. Bend over the lower edges and fold the overlapping edge on top, carefully gluing it on. By cautiously arching down one of the two folds inside the boat, you will create a boat that can float. You can also build this large folded boat into a large sailing ship or an 18th century or earlier ship.

You'll also need rectangular folding paper sheets of any size for making the small and large folded paper boats. As the folding directions on p. 52 show, crease the paper for the small folding ship so that you create an accordion fold (3). After that, the lower ends of the fold are bent strongly upward to the edge and creased thoroughly (4). After folding back and opening the ship slightly, the corners are pressed in (5) and glued together. This boat form can be readily transformed into a realistic boat. Nearly square paper will create rowboats and long rectangles will make canoes and kayaks. For the small folded boats in the harbor scene on p. 56, students chose bent cardboard strips for benches and rolled-up typing paper for oars or paddles. The blades were made out of colored paper.

SIMPLE BOAT

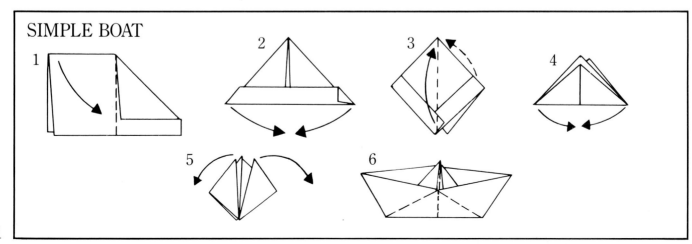

SMALL FOLDED BOAT

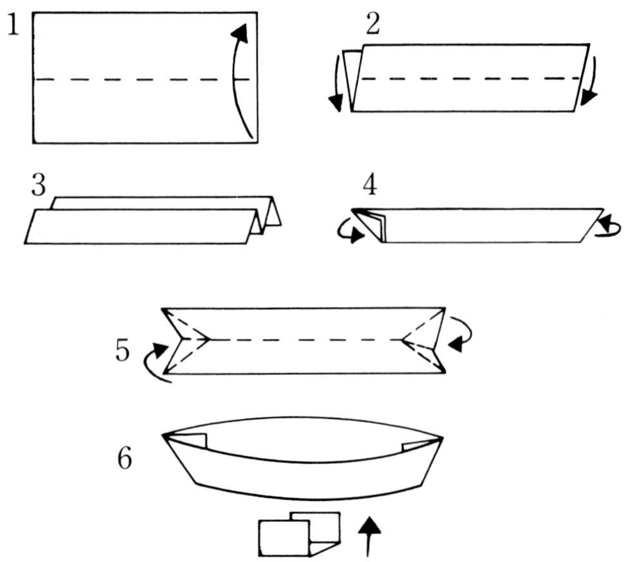

1

2

3

4

5

6

LARGE FOLDED BOAT

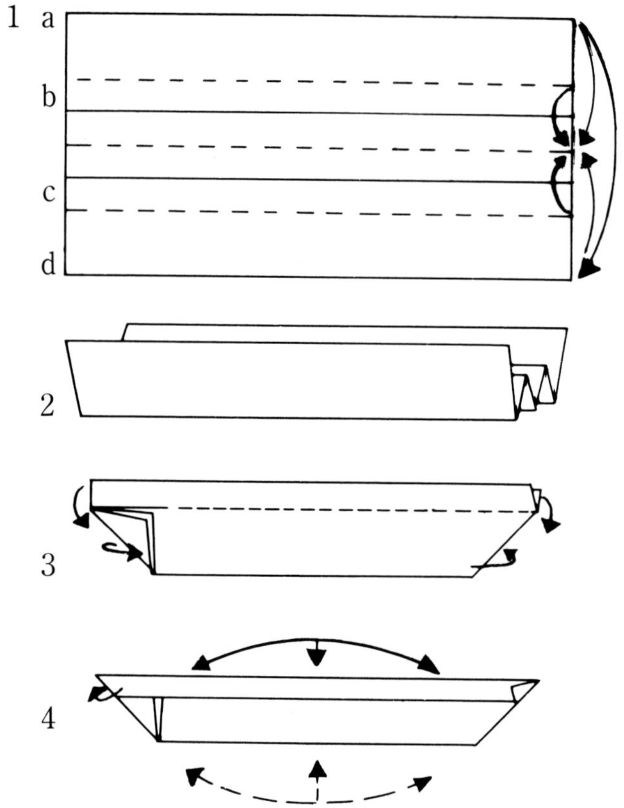

1 a

b

c

d

2

3

4

PUNCH PUPPET

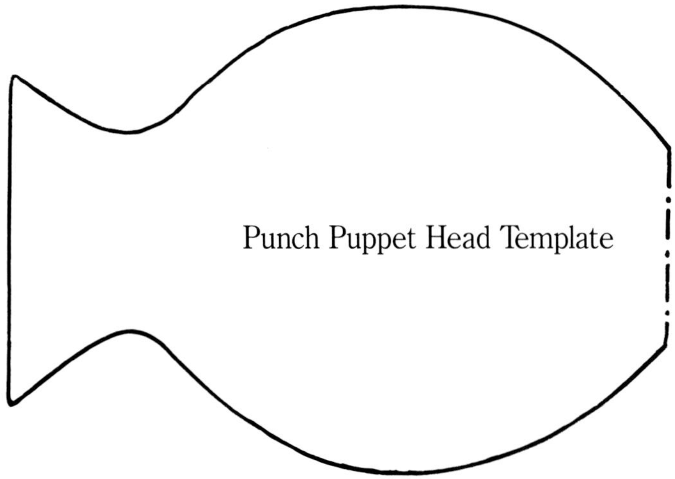

Punch Puppet Head Template

BAT

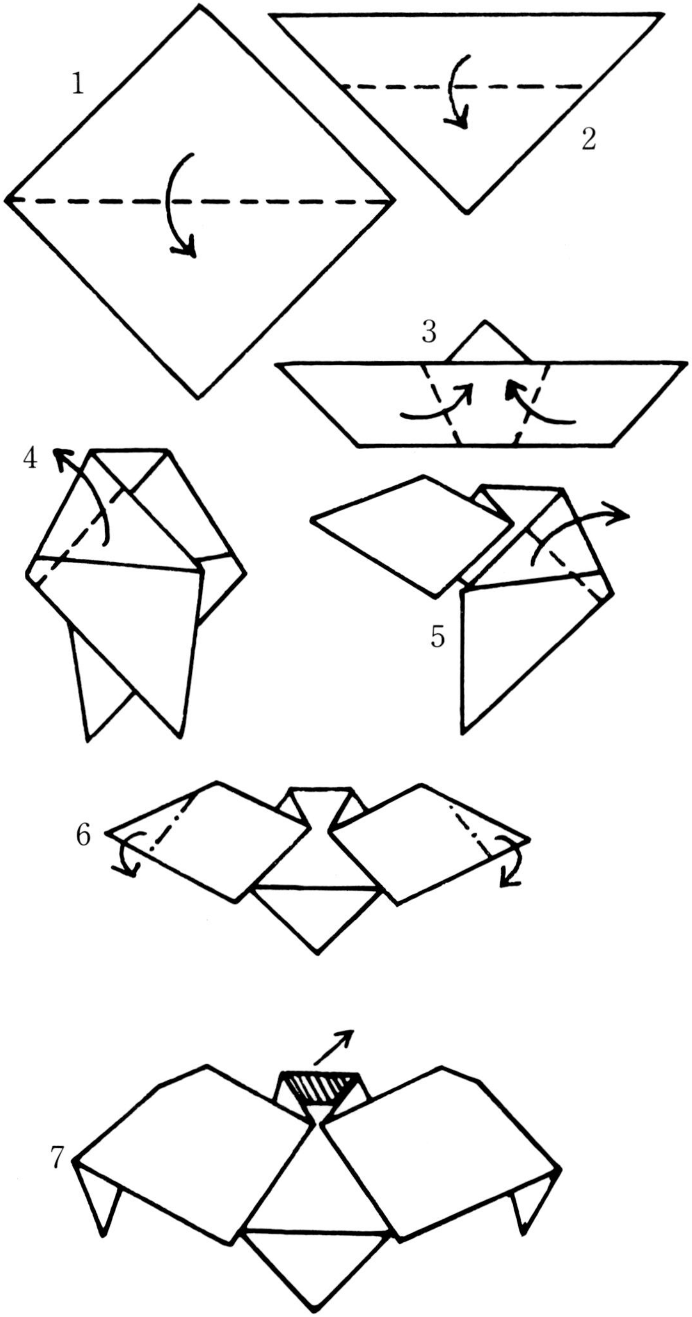

1

2

3

4

5

6

7

CROCODILE

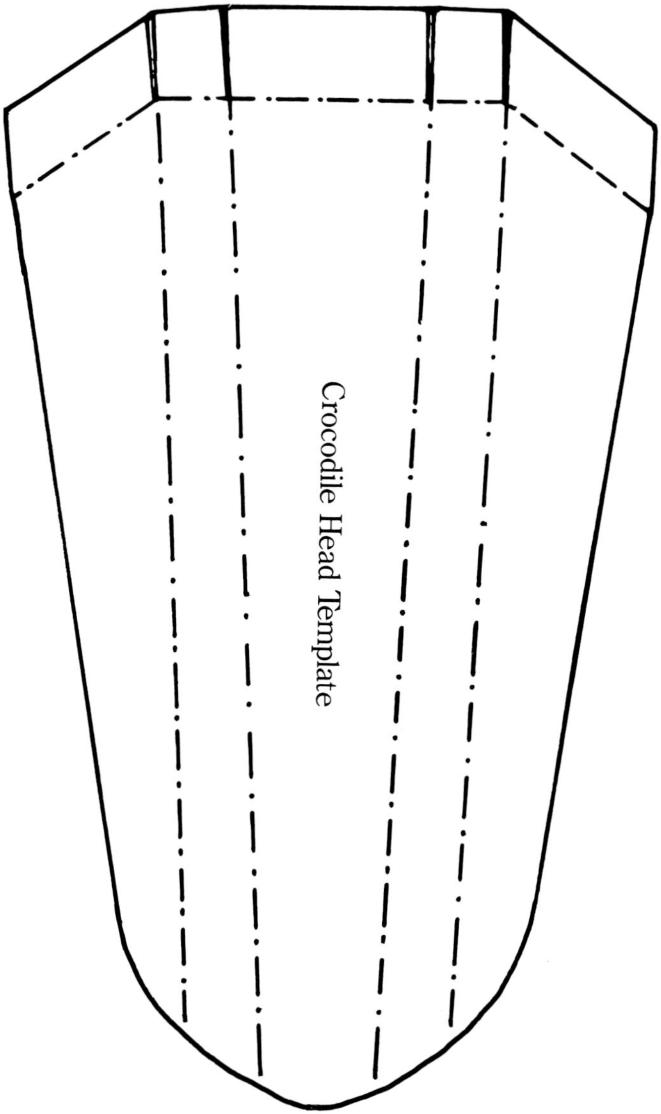

Crocodile Head Template

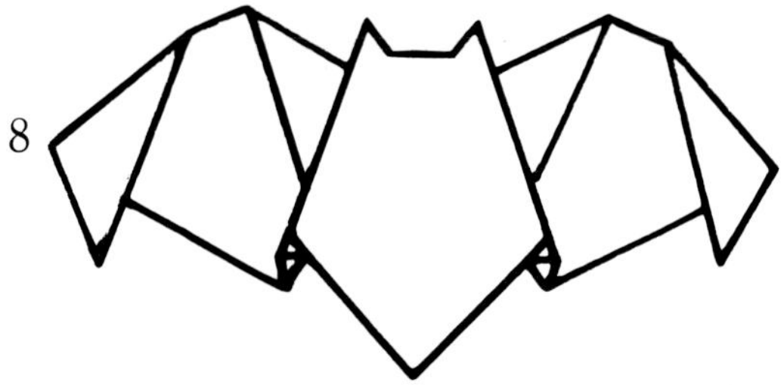

8

The Brave Tin Soldier   (p. 51)

54

55 *Landscape with Lake* *(p. 51)*

Boat Harbor   (p. 51)

Clacking Heads (p. 51)

More Folded Animals

include a dark blue paper background for sky and water. Find folding directions for the penguins below. Arrange them on the icebergs.

Penguins on Icebergs (p. 59)

Make the penguins on icebergs shown on the opposite page out of folding paper 4 inches (10 cm), 6 inches (15 cm), or 8 inches (20 cm) square. The paper used in the illustration is black on one side and white on the other. Add red glossy paper beaks, eyes of stickers, and an iceberg landscape made from broken Styrofoam pieces;

Bats against a Full Moon (p. 60)

The bats shown on p. 60 are especially effective posed in a dark night sky above folded and fringed fir trees. Here the larger bats fly low and the small bats high. Make the bats from paper squares 4 inches (10 cm), 6 inches (15 cm), and 8 inches (20 cm). Find folding directions for the bats on p. 53.

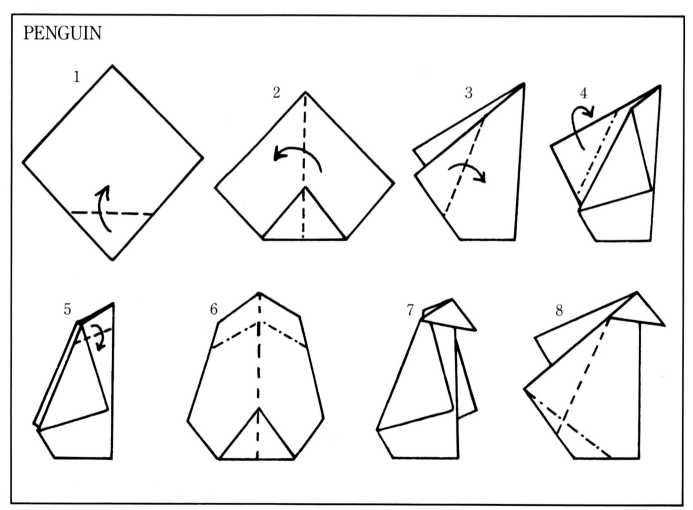

PENGUIN

Penguins on Icebergs *(p. 58)*

Bats against a Full Moon   *(p. 58)*

60

61　*Rooster, Hens, and Chickens in a Farmyard*　(p. 62)

Rooster, Hens, and Chickens in a Farmyard   (p. 61)

The yellow hens and chickens and the white rooster can be easily folded, although the two opposite folds for the head and the tail require some skill. It may take a little practice to coax the paper so that the chicken will stand up. Use yellow paper squares 3¼ inches (8 cm) and 4 inches (10 cm) for the hens and chickens, but 6 inches (15 cm) for the rooster. Decorate the hens, chickens, and rooster with colorful construction paper scraps. See folding directions on p. 63.

The brown hens and chickens require more folding steps, but except for bending the head forward, they can be made by younger children. Fold them out of 8-inch (20-cm) paper squares that are brown on both sides. See folding instructions on p. 63.

Create the landscape from wrapping paper and construction paper scraps.

Ducks and Swans Swimming   (cover)

Fold the ducks, which populate the idyllic landscape on the cover, out of yellow paper squares in three sizes— 4 inches (10 cm), 6 inches (15 cm), and 8 inches (20 cm). To make them look real, add a red rounded beak, pointed up a little, and glue the necks together underneath. Use a black felt-tip pen or self-adhesive circles for eye dots. Folding directions for the ducks are below.

The majestic swans can be easily folded out of 8-inch (20-cm) white paper squares. Also add red beaks with black rims and eye dots. Find folding directions for the swans on p. 64.

Create the landscape from wrapping paper and construction paper scraps.

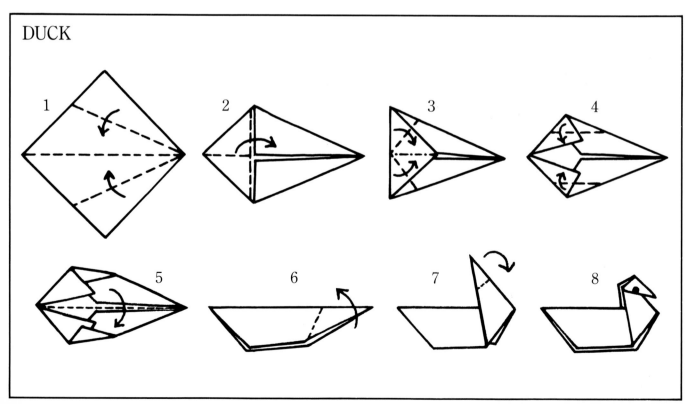

DUCK

BROWN HENS

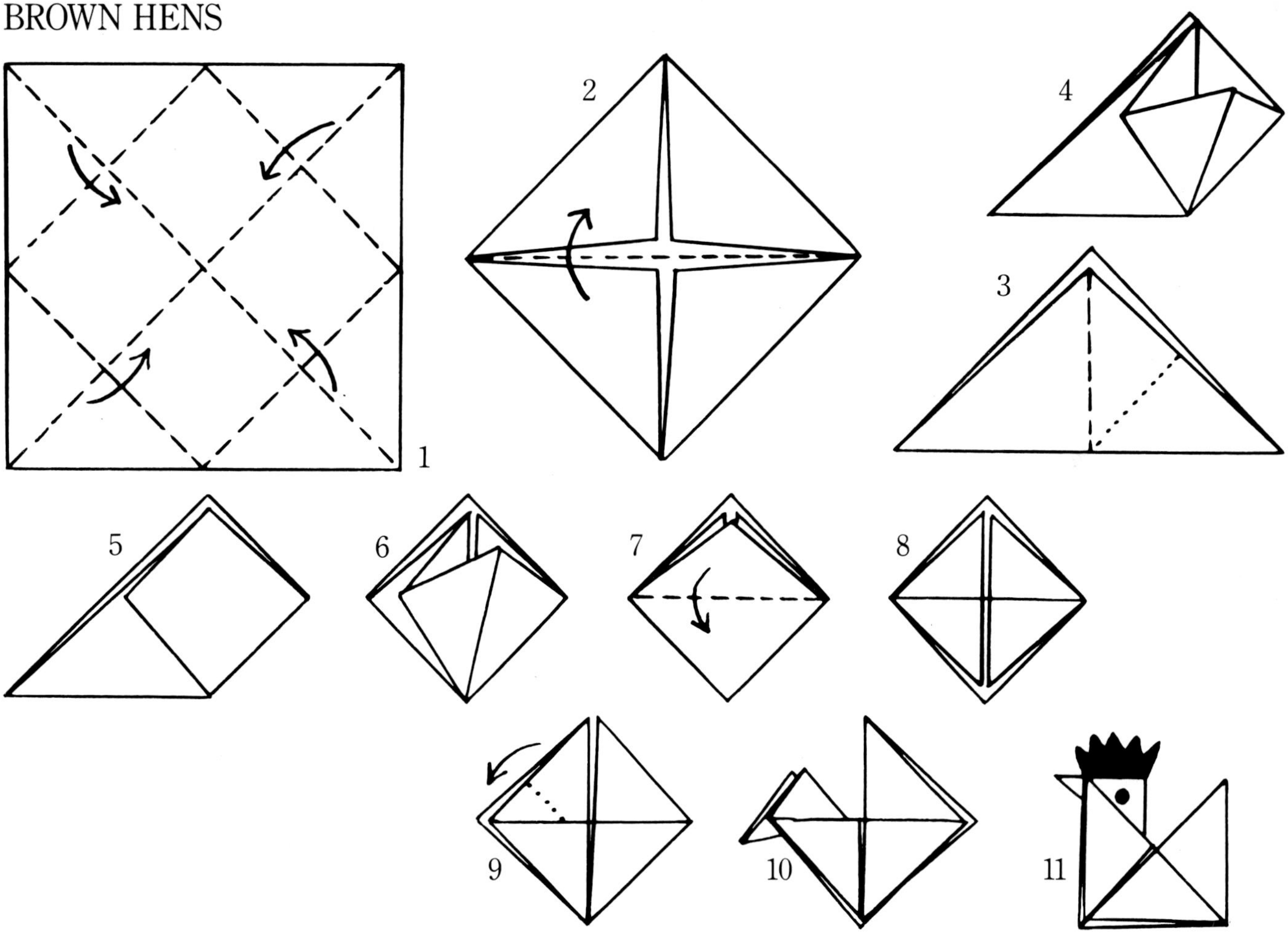

ROOSTER AND YELLOW HENS AND CHICKENS

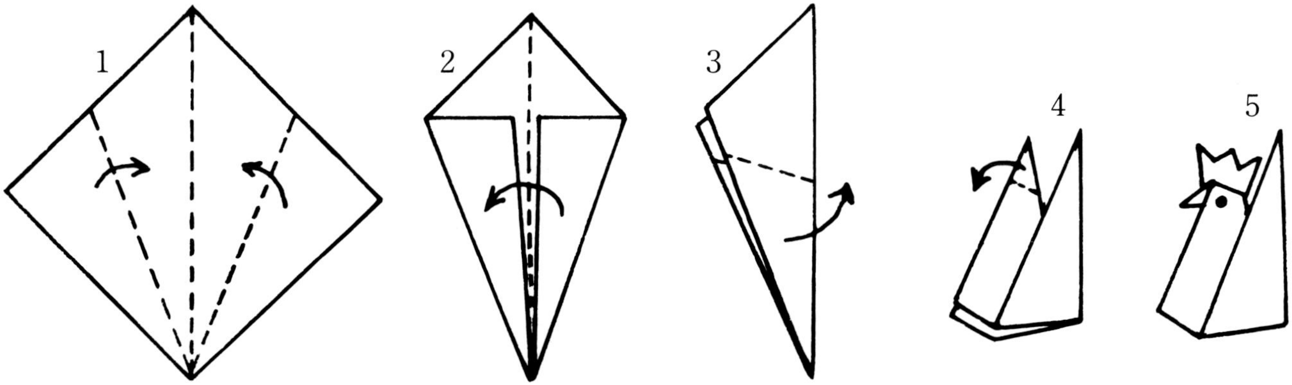

63

SWAN

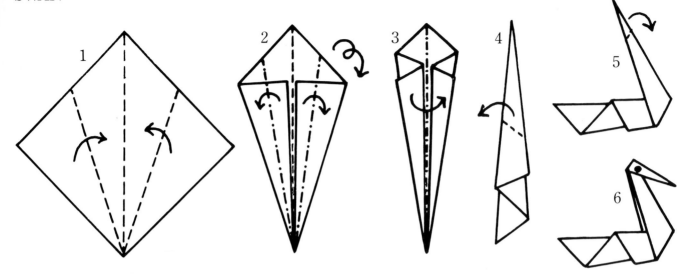

BREMEN TOWN MUSICIANS OR HAND PUPPETS

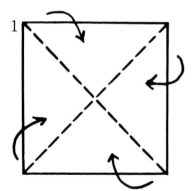

turn over and fold all corners toward the center

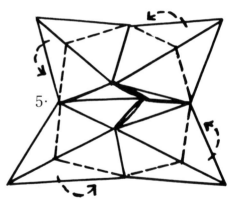

glue the two sides together

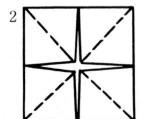

stick thumb and forefinger into the created square pockets, press into shape

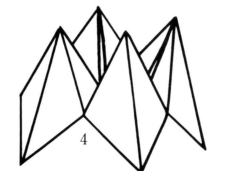

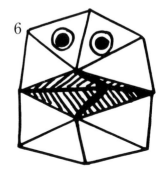

Bremen Town Musicians (p. 66)

The basic shape for the Bremen Town Musicians from the popular folktale is the small container, sometimes used as small table salt-and-pepper bowls at individual place settings. This versatile basic shape can also be used for making hand puppets of various descriptions; just decorate them appropriately. See basic folding directions on p. 64. Simply add colored paper cutouts for ears, whiskers, teeth, nose, or beard, as necessary. And pretty soon your musicians are ready.

Little Baskets (p. 67)

Follow a folding procedure with initial steps very similar to those for the Bremen Town Musicians to create the decorative and durable little baskets shown on p. 67. Begin with colored 12-inch (30-cm) paper squares. Colorful handles and construction paper decorations in compatible shades transform these little baskets into especially pretty table decorations. The little baskets shown could serve as party favors or even as baskets for Easter goodies.

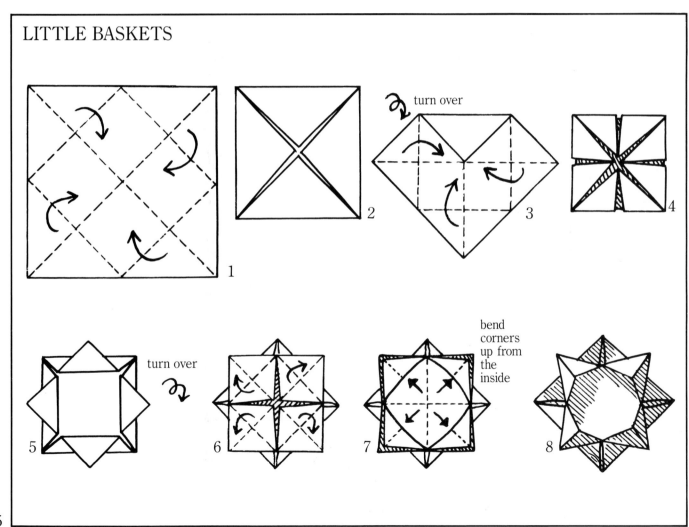

LITTLE BASKETS

Bremen Town Musicians (p. 65)

66

Little Baskets (p. 65)

Holland Landscape (p. 68)

The Holland landscape, complete with windmills, tulips, and boats shown below draws on a few basic folded shapes. Glue two identical shapes on top of each other and shift them to create the distinctive windmill blades. The windmills appear three-dimensional, since the towers that support them are folded and cut before they were glued on the Holland montage shown below. See folding directions for the windmill on p. 69.

The tulips shown below were folded according to directions for Tulip II shown on p. 69. A simple tulip can also be made by folding the sides over and then folding the lower corners up. Also see Tulip I folding directions on p. 69. Then plant them in hillsides of construction paper and fabric with leaves and grasses.

For the simple folded sailboats (illustration's lower right corner) see folding directions on p. 46. And for the small folded boats (lower left corner of illustration), see p. 51.

Holland Landscape *(p. 68)*

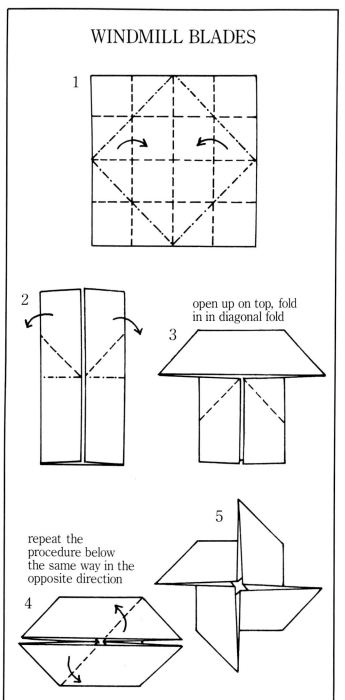

WINDMILL BLADES

1

2

3

open up on top, fold
in in diagonal fold

repeat the
procedure below
the same way in the
opposite direction

4

5

TULIPS

Tulip I

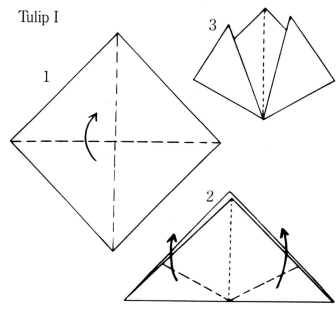

1

3

2

Tulip II

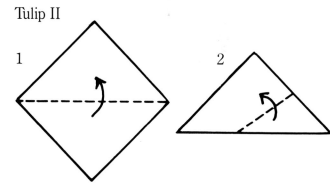

1

2

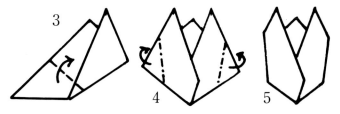

3

4

5

Santa Comes through the Forest, an Advent Calendar   (p. 71)

Looking a Lot Like Christmas

Santa Comes through the Forest, an Advent Calendar (p. 70)

For this Advent calendar, Santa Claus Comes through the Forest, second-graders used drawing paper and crayons to draw pine trees, mushrooms, rabbits, deer, and sleds, as well as Santa and the angels. These figures were cut out and placed against a black background.

The numbered presents contain tiny surprises inside. One present (envelope) is opened on each of the days of Advent up until Christmas. The presents were made from the versatile drinking cup shape. See folding directions on this page. Ribbons were drawn on and numbers added on round stickers.

Saint Nicholas in a Winter Landscape (p. 72)

When Saint Nicholas steps right out of the snow-covered forest into our room it seems a lot like Christmas. Saint Nick's long red coat is made out of the bell shape (see folding directions on p. 17) and basic form II (see folding directions on p. 6). Begin with a red 12-inch (30-cm) paper square for the skirt, and a red 6-inch (15-cm) paper square for the cape. Fold the face, beard, and cap out of a glossy 3¼-inch (8-cm) paper square, following folding directions below. Insert a triangular skin-colored paper for the face (see pattern on p. 73). Draw or cut out paper eyes, nose, mouth, and moustache. Cut out paper mittens and glue them inside his sleeves.

Also find the pattern for Saint Nicholas's staff on p. 73. Cut it out of cardboard and cover it with gold foil. Make the bag that holds presents following the folding directions for Red Riding Hood's cap, but begin with an 8-inch (20-cm) paper square. See folding directions on p. 30.

Stuff crumpled-up tissue paper in the finished bag; tie the sack with a thin gold string.

The snow-covered Christmas trees complete the wintry scene. Begin with dark green paper squares 9 inches (23 cm), 8¼ inches (21 cm), 7½ inches (19 cm), 6¾ inches (17 cm), and 6 inches (15 cm). Fold them into basic form I (see p. 6). Then fold white paper squares about ½ inch (1 cm) bigger than the green branches and cut them out for the snow. Pile finished branch and snow on branch and snow to the desired height. Keep the largest branches at the bottom and top the tree with successively smaller branches.

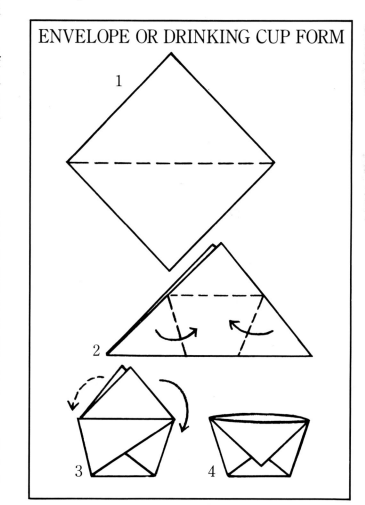

ENVELOPE OR DRINKING CUP FORM

Saint Nicholas in a Winter Landscape   (p. 73)

SAINT NICHOLAS

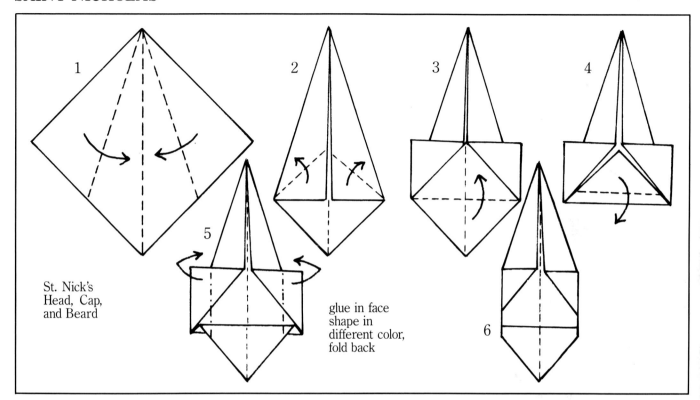

1

St. Nick's
Head, Cap,
and Beard

2

glue in face
shape in
different color,
fold back

3

4

5

6

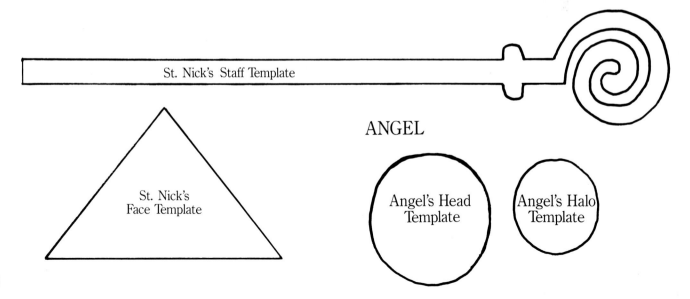

St. Nick's Staff Template

St. Nick's
Face Template

ANGEL

Angel's Head
Template

Angel's Halo
Template

Red Christmas Trees   (p. 18)

74

Angels and Bells (p. 18)

Starry Angels (p. 77)

Starry Angels (p. 76)

The simple angels shown on the opposite page can serve as Christmas ornaments or can decorate Christmas cards. They will even stand up by themselves if you simply bend the three skirt parts back and forward. They will add sparkle to each table setting decorated in the spirit of Christmas. These angels can be quickly folded and glued together.

Create the three skirt shapes out of foil paper 2¼ inches by 4 inches (6 cm by 10 cm), the upper body from 1½-inch-by-2½-inch (4-cm-by-6½-cm) paper, and the wings from three pieces 1¼ inches by 2 inches (3 cm by 5 cm). Fold parts for the skirt, upper body, and wings into the basic kite form below. Also see p. 79 for folding assembly directions and find patterns for head and halo on p. 73. The little angels look especially nice when they're made in matching shades but with different kinds of shiny paper. Experiment a little.

If you like, you can extend the angel's skirt, making eight or more kite shapes to make foil stars. Just attach them in the center at the narrowest part.

These angel skirts and wings make the rays of stars when placed pointy side out.

Transparent Stars (p. 78)

The large folded stars on p. 78 are made out of transparent paper. They can sparkle in every window at Christmas or help decorate a New Year's party or birthday party. They consist of eight to sixteen paper rays 3¼ inches by 5 inches (8 cm by 13 cm) or 2½ inches by 4 inches (6 cm by 10 cm). See folding directions for the stars on p. 79.

When the stars are assembled with wide parts of the folded kite form in the center or when the individual rays or kite forms are unfolded halfway, eight folded kite forms are sufficient. Of course, the star with sixteen rays is even more brilliant when rays overlap and the papers used are transparent. The best effect can be achieved by hanging the finished star in a window, where light can shine through.

Foil stars (not shown) can be folded and glued together just like these large transparent stars. They can make pretty table decorations, tree ornaments, or even Christmas cards, when attached to a folded card shape. Use foil that's 2½ inches by 4 inches (6 cm by 10 cm), 1½ inches by 2½ inches (4 cm by 6½ cm), and 1¼ inches by 2 inches (3 cm by 5 cm). The smallest stars fit on paper Christmas cards.

SIMPLE KITE SHAPE

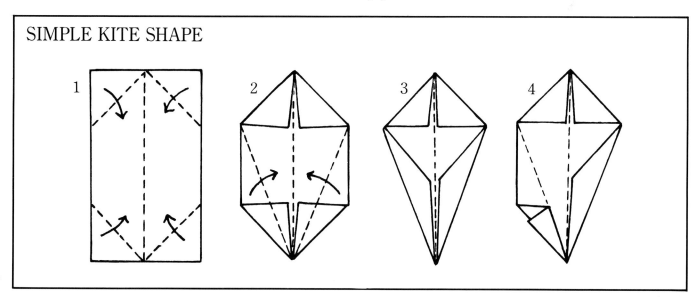

Transparent Stars   *(p. 77)*